# ARE THERE COPPER PIPES IN HEAVEN

# ERU KOPARRØR Í HIMMIRÍKI

POEMS BY KATRIN OTTARSDÓTTIR

TRANSLATIONS BY MATTHEW LANDRUM
WITH SÁMAL SOLL

the operating system print//document

# ARE THERE COPPER PIPES IN HEAVEN
## ERU KOPARRØR Í HIMMIRÍKI

ISBN: 978-1-946031-59-4
Library of Congress Control Number: 2019947984
copyright © 2020 by Matthew Landrum / Katrin Ottarsdóttir
edited and designed by ELÆ [Lynne DeSilva-Johnson]

with additional typesetting by Janice Lee
and cover design assistance by Zoe Guttenplan

is released under a Creative Commons CC-BY-NC-ND (Attribution, Non Commercial, No Derivatives) License: its reproduction is encouraged for those who otherwise could not afford its purchase in the case of academic, personal, and other creative usage from which no profit will accrue.

Complete rules and restrictions are available at:
http://creativecommons.org/licenses/by-nc-nd/3.0/

For additional questions regarding reproduction, quotation, or to request a pdf for review contact operator@theoperatingsystem.org

*This text was set in Europa, Minion, Freight Sans, Franchise, Gill Sans, and OCR-A Standard.*

Books from The Operating System are distributed to the trade via Ingram, with additional production by Spencer Printing.

## the operating system
www.theoperatingsystem.org

# ARE THERE COPPER PIPES IN HEAVEN

## ERU KOPARRØR Í HIMMIRÍKI

# TABLE OF CONTENTS

| | |
|---|---:|
| TRANSLATOR'S PREFACE | 7 |
| HAVI / GARDEN | 12 |
| HÚS / HOUSE | 14 |
| SKÁP / CUPBOARD | 16 |
| VEGGIR / WALLS | 18 |
| SPROYTUR / NEEDLES | 20 |
| LYKLAR / KEYS | 24 |
| LUDO / LUDO | 28 |
| SJÁLVMORÐIÐ / THE SUICIDE | 32 |
| MYNDIR / PICTURES | 36 |
| RABARBUGREYTUR / RHUBARB STEW | 40 |
| MÁNI / MOON | 48 |
| SÓL / SUN | 56 |
| SJÁLVMORÐIÐ / THE SUICIDE | 58 |
| ERU KOPARRØR Í HIMMIRÍKI / ARE THERE COPPER PIPES IN HEAVEN | 62 |
| OSTASKORPUR / CHEESE RINDS | 66 |
| 13 ÁR / 13 YEARS | 68 |
| ISTEDGADE / ISTEDGADE | 72 |
| SKÁK OG MÁT / CHECK MATE | 78 |
| SJÁLVMORÐIÐ / THE SUICIDE | 80 |
| SMÍL / SMILE | 82 |
| TEY DEYÐU / THE DEAD | 84 |
| ÚTVARP / RADIO | 88 |
| LÍKAMIKIÐ / NEVERMIND | 90 |
| ACKNOWLEDGEMENTS | 93 |
| BREAKING OPEN THE LONG DARK / Q&A | 94 |

# TRANSLATOR'S PREFACE

"I do not know that she should have written it."

It was 2016 and I was in The Faroe Islands working on a translation grant for Katrin Ottarsdóttir's book *Are there Copper Pipes in Heaven*. I would often hear some iteration of that sentiment when I mentioned my project.

Ottarsdóttir's debut collection breaks ground in Faroese literature. It is the first book of confessional poetry in Faroese and it's difficult material — domestic abuse, drug abuse, mental illness, and coming of age in a conservative culture — breaks social mores in this close-knit society.

With a capital of 21,000 and a total population on the archipelago that just broke 50,000, the Faroe Islands are essentially a small town. Everyone is related within a few degrees. Privacy is closely guarded. Emotions are kept in check. Though global trends are bringing a greater expressiveness to Faroese language, it's still high praise to be told "that's not so bad."

As an award winning writer and the pre-eminent Faroese filmmaker — her films *Atlantic Rhapsody* and *Bye Bye Bluebird* are foundational to Faroese filmmaking — her influence is far-reaching. And her treatment of the subject matter is thorough. If people didn't read the book, there's also a movie. The book's material is re-explored in her 2014 film *Ludo* with Ottarsdóttir's daughter playing her mother. There was even an interactive art installation at the Norðurlandahúsið in 2012. Exhibit goers would move from room to room hearing shouting voices from other rooms. "That was too much for me," one friend said of it.

Another, speaking of the book, told me, "My parents knew her parents and they saw the situation differently."

I shared these responses with Katrin at a Copenhagen cafe a few years later. She nodded. "My father was a beloved educator and respected in town." She explained that the public face of the family was very different from what went on behind the walls of the family's house.

The book presents a narrow world where cycles of abuse and appeasement play out between mother, father, and child. The focus on this family of three (the father, the mother, and the child) — what Ottarsdóttir calls "the trinity" — is nearly exclusive. The only other figures in the book are a group of prostitutes, drug-pushing doctors, Neil Armstrong, the disembodied voice of Leonard Cohen, a dog, and a bunch of anthropomorphic rhubarb. It is the only Faroese book I know of that does not mention the sea.

Ottarsdóttir's tumultuous trinity of mother, father, and child is the central organizing motif of the book. Each has its own niche which extends even to the book's grammar. Faroese, like other Scandinavian languages, is gendered. A boat is female, the gallbladder is neuter, snow is masculine and Faroese speakers use pronouns for each noun accordingly. This is simple enough with the father — *he* — and the mother — *she*. But in Faroese, child is a neuter noun with the corresponding pronoun *it*. Early on in the project, I defaulted to English habits and translated the child's pronouns *she/her/hers*. But when I sent my initial draft to Ottarsdóttir, she wrote back that only the mother could be referred to as she — a pronoun for each godhead of the trinity. So what to do? Calling a preteen girl "it" in English is unthinkable. It conjured up my childhood and my older sister's bookshelf with its copy of the 1995 bestseller A Child Called It. That wouldn't do. After some discussion and casting about, I decided to lean into new pronoun usages in English, specifically for the singular use of "they" which, to me, best conveys the non-gendered connotation of the Faroese "tað" without the dehumanizing qualities of the English "it."

The book's opening poem captures a brief moment of calm. The father is tending his backyard garden. Here he is the master of his domain, tending and pruning, plucking and protecting. Everything he touches grows. He matters; he is self-contained. The poem ends with him heading back into the house where a storm is brewing. Here, his confidence and competence is stripped away. He is at the whim of a mentally unstable spouse, vacillating between frenetic appeasement and dejected isolation. He enters into asymmetric power games, allowed to flirt with workers in the red light district in Copenhagen until being yanked back to reality by his wife's mood. He cooks her favorite dessert in hopes of making her happy only to have his hopes dashed by her complaints about the mess in the kitchen. She mentally and physically abuses him, even going so far as attacking him with kitchen knives. He sometimes responds physically but most often retreats to the narrow basement. The title poem, "Are there Copper Pipes in Heaven," depicts him trapped in the basement as his wife goes around the house turning on every faucet and flushing the toilets so the sharp rush of water through the plumbing will torment him and ensure he doesn't get a moment's rest.

Imperious and completely unpredictable, the mother's mood reigns over the household. There's no telling what will set off a crisis. A look or glance could be misinterpreted. Her husband stewing rhubarb for her as a special treat will be met with joy one time and rage the next. She threatens suicide and self-medicates. Three poems called "The Suicide" punctuate the book, relating the constant spector of suicide haunting the child, lurking in every corner, and controlling everything. She keeps a spotless house with chic decor, all signs of struggle and domestic life carefully straightened and dusted away. But her vision for perfection is continually marred by her instability and by her husband and child. The child, unwanted and unwelcome, in particular doesn't fit into her life. She resents the child, thinking her husband loves them more than her. She needs and despises her husband, pitching and yawing between vitriol and sexual want, uncontrolled rage and playing house.

Raised in the tidal rhythms of the house, the child becomes caretaker and mediator. They are always playing the middle trying to maintain the shaky peace of the household and make sure their mother doesn't follow through on her many threats of suicide. They make themselves as small as possible and tiptoe through the house, seeing violent abuse and violent makeup sex, all the while neglected, an afterthought. They are a sort of Greek chorus, witness to a tragedy, profoundly affected but powerless to change the situation. The child is a pest to the mother and, though loved, an afterthought to the father in his own struggle to cope.

But children do not stay children. In the first poems, there is only a ghostly presence of a child playing hide and seek in the house, forgotten, alone, and afraid. Time passes and the child begins to ask why and try to mediate the tensions of the house. Neil Armstrong walks on the moon. The family moves house. The child discovers Leonard Cohen. Their period starts. The narrative arc moves toward adulthood but age doesn't bring freedom. Ottarsdóttir imagines that not even death can free us from fraught relationships. She images the dead "waiting for a chance to tell you / what a fucker you are / how fucking useless you've always been." Home is something you carry with you, even to the afterlife.

Ottarsdóttir's 1999 film *Bye, Bye Bluebird*, a classic of Faroese cinematography, tells the story of two punk rock women returning to Tórshavn after living in mainland Europe. Their homecoming leads to tensions and conflicts with the sleepy conservatism of 1990's Faroese culture that doesn't know what to do with their dramatic hairstyles, dark makeup, and grunge attitudes. I see this book as analogous to that narrative. Ottarsdóttir, who lives in Copenhagen, returned to the material of childhood and home, writing a book that pushes against prevailing privacy norms.

But there is another analogy I prefer for this book. 55 million years ago, a fault opened between the Eurasian and North American plates. A violent upheaval of volcanism followed, creating the Faroe Islands.

From upheaval, comes creation. It is precisely at such points of tension and unrest, volcanic as they sometimes are — that great art is born. *Are there Copper Pipes in Heaven* is a product of fault lines, both personal and culture, the surface pulled apart to make new ground, raw, difficult, and beautiful.

*Matthew Landrum*
*Detroit — September, 2019*

# HAVI

dreymarnir brotna í vøkrum havum
ein rhododendron kveylar leivdirnar í seg
gevur maðkunum enn eina grund at vera til

suffini fara millum havarnar
leita eftir meiningini í mjúku moldini
undir blóðdropunum hjá kristusi
heldur ikki hann veit síni livandi ráð

í einum hava grør alt sum maðurin nertir
hjartað lekur innistongd orð út í fingrarnar
allir litir leskiliga lokkandi
inni í húsinum er útideyðaveður
skjótt noyðist hann at fara inn

## GARDEN

dreams decompose in the back gardens
rhododendrons grow fat on the compost
and worms find yet another reason to exist

sighs run between the rows
searching for meaning in the soft loam
beneath fuchsia flowers
that look like drops of christ's blood
even he's at his wits end

everything in the garden the man touches grows
his heart leaching what he can't say through his fingers
the colors are so vibrant so bewitching
but there's a storm brewing in the house
and soon he'll have to go back inside

# HÚS

eitt hús
seks úthurðar
seytjan innihurðar
trýogtjúgu lyklarhol

so nógvar hurðar at læsa
so nógvar hurðar at sparka
og bresta upp og aftur
men tað slapp bara ein
hon
ikki hann
ikki barnið

so nógv lyklarhol
so nógvir næstan sama slag lyklar
men barnið kendi ikki lyklarnar
bara hon
onkuntíð hann

hurðar inn til grát og tannagrísl
ørandi máttloysi ekkóandi gjøgnum lyklarholini
syngjandi leysir hurðaklædningar fullir av forbannilsum
nætur fullar av innistongdum hurðaljóðum
men ongir lyklar

so nógvar hurðar
álíkavæl mátti hann fara út gjøgnum vindeygað í kjallaranum
sama vindeygað hvørja ferð
undir trappuni har ongin sá
tað var jú skomm

men eftir stóð barnið

# HOUSE

a house
six doors outside
seventeen doors inside
twenty-three keyholes

so many doors to lock
so many doors to kick
and slam open or shut
only one of them was allowed to do that
only she
not he
and not the child

so many keyholes
so many near-identical keys
but the child didn't know which was which
only she
and sometimes he

doors leading to wailing and gnashing of teeth
heady impotence echoing through the keyholes
the cursing of feet against a rickety hollow core door
nights full of the pent-up sounds of doors
without keys

so many doors
still he had to climb through the basement window
the same window every time
under the stairs where nobody could see him
after all it was a disgrace

and he left the child behind

## SKÁP

nervapillarar ringla í skápum
fáa skápshurðar at ríkja
lógvar at fyllast og tømast
tenn at gresja beiska smakkin av lívinum

pillararnir eiga hetta lívið
læknin er millummaður
millum guð og devulin og trongdina

harrin lurtar ikki longur
menniskjan ræðist alt

## CUPBOARD

nerve pills rattle in cupboards
and cabinet doors creak open
palms fill and empty
teeth grind down life's bitterness

the pills control existence here
between god and the devil and the urge
the doctor plays middleman

the lord isn't listening any longer
and mankind has everything to fear

# VEGGIR

vónin situr í veggjunum í húsunum
har tárini
øðin
pínan
hava valdið

gleðin er friðleys
saman við stívnaðu smílunum trampar hon rútmuna
í ørliga dansinum í myrku rúmunum
nátt og dag
so børn gerast vaksin áðrenn sólin rísur
og vaksin aftur missa álitið á sær sjálvum

vónloysið er besti vinur hjá møðini
saman skapa tey máttloysi
sum uttan náði fær sær sess í húsunum
so hann og hon
ikki longur orka at síggja barnið
sum situr inni í veggjunum og bíðar eftir teimum

## WALLS

hope sits in the walls
of the house
where tears
pain
rage
hold sway

joy is an outlaw here
with stiff smiles it stamps out its rhythm
a mad dance in darkened rooms
night and day
so that children become adults before the sun rises
and adults lose faith in themselves all over again

despair makes friends with fatigue
together they create an impotence
which mercilessly takes seat in the house
so that he and she
can no longer bear to see the child
sitting in the walls waiting for them

## SPROYTUR

móðir læknar við tómum eygum
taskum fullum av gloymsku

sproytur sproyta alla náttina
blankar nálir ið uttan at himprast
finna sær veg til æðrar fullar av migrenu og forbannilsi
æðrar sum bara bíða eftir morfinundrinum

sum antin

fer at sláa beinini undan henni
so hon blindað av ringum tannabiti
má grulva allan vegin út á kummuna
og goysa gor og gall
og vit og skil
og fedranna syndir
úr sær

ella

fer at geva henni purpurlitta friðin
fáa hana at sova so helvitisliga deiligt og ævinliga leingi
og gloyma alt um bleikar risthentar læknar við ringum anda
og um hann og barnið
sum bara duga at halda ondini
meðan tey bíða eftir at morfineingilin skal bretta sær á
og reka illu andarnar úr húsinum
og úr øllum æðrum
fullum av stórslignari pínu
og vánaligum lívi

# NEEDLES

tired doctors with empty eyes
and medical bags full of oblivion

syringes plunge through the night
blank needles unerringly hit
veins full of migraines and imprecations
veins waiting for the morphine wonder

that will either

knock her back on her heels
leaving her blind with hate
groping her way to the toilet on hands and knees
to puke out her guts
and senses
and the sins of
her fathers

or

give her that violet peace
and make her sleep so fucking lovely and everlong
and forget about doctors with shaky hands and bad breath
and about the man and the child
who know nothing but how to hold their breath
as they wait for the morphine angel to spread its wings
and chase the demons out of the house
out of every vein
full of agony
and domestic failure

læknarnir suffa inniliga og vaska sær
enn einaferð um hendurnar inni á tí grøna vesinum

álvarsamir menn og álvarsamar kvinnur
sum ikki vilja síggja ella skilja veruliga standin
í húsunum hjá pínuni
yvir allar pínur

and the doctors sigh and wash their hands
in the green-tiled bathroom

grave men and grave women
that don't want to see what life is really like
in this house of pain
to end all pain

# LYKLAR

óteljandi hurðar
sum noyddu hann
at fara út gjøgnum vindeygað tá hann vildi út
heilt út

hóttandi hurðar
millum hann
og hana og eydnuna
og so barnið
á hatta ólukksáliga barnið

hurðar at fara út ígjøgnum
og aldrin koma aftur
aftur
sum av torvheiðum tá verðin gálvar og gleivar
og vil verða tikin her og nú
og menniskju svølta og verða dripin
og ikki hava ráð til lyklar og salt

soleiðis hugsaði barnið
og hugdi út gjøgnum vindeygað
eftir fótafetum í kavanum
sum langt síðani var horvin

hurðar at steingja
við illsintum dýrgoldnum lyklum
ið aldrin passa niður í smáar barnalummar
tí hurðarnar steingja báðar vegir
allar vegir
inneftir og úteftir
frameftir og aftureftir

# KEYS

numberless doors
forced him
to climb out the window
when he wanted out
all the way out

implacable doors
stood between him
and her and joy
and then the child
that damn child

doors to pass through
and never return
again
empty handed when the world sticks out its tongue
and spreads its legs for you
and wants to be taken right then and there
and all the while people are starving
and getting murdered
and can't afford keys or salt

or so the child thought
looking out the window
for footprints
long since vanished in the snow

doors to lock
with jangling keys that came at a price
but never fit into a child's small pockets
because doors lock both ways
every way

at koma á stongdar dyr
hevði ein serligan týdning í hesum húsinum

fara vit nú
spurdi barnið
um hurðin vil
svaraði hann

hon segði onki
tí lyklarnir larmaðu so illa
og beint tá
var harrin ikki harri yvir lyklunum longur

einaferð fór barnið
og mundi ikki funnið aftur
aftur

from the inside and outside
backwards and forwards

to come to a locked door
meant something in that house

can we go now
asked the child
if the door lets us
he answered

she didn't reply
because the keys were so loud
and in that moment
the lord was no longer lord of the keys

once the child left
and almost couldn't find their way
back again
from the inside and outside
backwards and forwards

## LUDO

tey klemmast á køksgólvinum
hann
og hon
øðin er uppi fyri hesa ferð
klandrið seyrar út gjøgnum veggirnar
niður í gólvið

barnið stendur bara har
hyggur
heldur ondini
sleppur álíkavæl upp í klemmið í nátt
vil
vil ikki
spæla spælið longur

um eina løtu kemur møðin
og ludospælið undir lampuni
har náttin ræður
á reyða voksdúkinum

tey lata tankarnar ansa eftir hvørjum øðrum
spælið er ikki bara spæl
eitt heilt annað spæl
vandamikið spæl
ikki ludospæl
deyðiligt veruleikaspæl sum hvørja løtu kann bresta

eitt eygnabrá
eitt hirs
eitt andaleyst geisp
eitt skroypiligt pápaeyga ið næstan smílist
ein barnslig gnisan sum vardi ov stutt

# LUDO

they embrace on the kitchen floor
he
and she
her fury has passed for now
the quarrel that seeped through the walls
and into the floor

the child just stands there
watching
hardly breathing
they are allowed a goodnight hug
they want
but don't want to
play the game anymore

at any moment fatigue will hit
and end the game of ludo beneath the kitchen lamp
where darkness holds sway
over the red wax tablecloth

all of them let their thoughts keep watch
the game is more than a game
an entirely different game
a dangerous game
no longer a game of ludo
but a deadly game of reality set to explode

a look
a tic
a breathless yawn
a father's fragile eyes almost smiling
a childish giggle that lasts too long

ov leingi
kann senda alt til helvitis so hurðar aftur smekka
og okkurt aftur brotnar
uttan um tey
innan í teimum

og so sita tey aftur har
hann og barnið
og hava so ilt í búkinum
meðan náttin flennir

or too briefly
can send it all to hell so that doors slam again
and make things break
around them
inside them

so here they sit once more
he and the child
sick to their stomachs
as the night laughs

# SJÁLVMORÐIÐ

sjálvmorðið ballar barnið
um kvøldini tá sólin smílandi fer í kav

norðurættin grætur suðureftir

sjálvmorðið luktar
sum bara ein mamma kann lukta

sjálvmorðið er eisini við í dupultsongini
hjá henni
og honum
í explorasjónskreminum
í tubuni sum skelvandi hendur
kroysta út í treingjandi kyn
sum aldrin fær nokk

tann dagin barnið av óvart letur hurðina upp
sær hann oman á henni
kennir ræðsluslignu øðina frá honum fossa ímóti sær
veit barnið knappliga
hví sjálvmorðið býr har í húsunum
saman við teimum

stillisliga
sum er tað ikki til
letur barnið hurðina aftur
heldur ondini
líka til sjálvmorðið aftur
hevur ballað barnið væl og virðiliga
signað tað so vælsignað

## THE SUICIDE

the suicide envelopes the child
in evenings when the sun sets smilingly

the northern wind cries southerly

the suicide smells
as only a mother can smell

the suicide's
hers
and his
as trembling hands
squeeze ky jelly
into needy palms
that can never get enough

one day the child accidentally opened the door
and saw him on top of her
and felt his terrible fury pouring against her
and then the child understood
why the suicide lived in the house
with them

quietly
as if they didn't exist
the child closed the door
holding their breath
until the suicide thoroughly
wrapped them up again
blessing them thoroughly

nú er bara dreymaleysa náttin eftir
vælsignað av einglum sum enn einaferð leggja alt í sor

sjálvmorðið ringir fyri oyrunum
áðrenn sólin aftur rísur
og rekur søtu dreymarnar niður og norður

now only the sleepless night remains
blessed by angels that once again destroy everything

the suicide is ringing in their ears
before the sun rises once more
and drives their sweet dreams to hell

## MYNDIR

lívið er støvað av
10 ruddiligar myndir
15 × 11 cm í snøggum brúnum albummi
við gulllittum snóri úr silki
svart-hvítt lív í gráum
steðgað upp í leicaoptikki

hon leikstjórnar við magasýrukendum stílmedviti
hann spælir glaðiliga við sum stand-in í sínum egna lívi
uttan at merkja ósjónliga barnið
sum andøvir allastaðni í luftini rundan um tey
pinnastilt andandi í fínasta skrúð
eygleiðandi myndirnar
fyri ikki at gloyma alt um ruddilig lív

kanska er barnið akkurát tá í kjallaranum og biður eftir
at kosmiski fotografurin fer avstað aftur
syngur innantanna líka til tað verður
borið upp aftur í hitan
við heimleysu luktunum

barnið er ongastaðni og allastaðni og ongastaðni
ongi barnslig spor síggjast í ruddiligheitini
ongin gloymd dukka liggur og amast upp at svørtum metalbeinum
á strongum teakborðum við søholm vasum

onki lego sløðist dovisliga á gráum arabarapútum
sum í veruleikanum eru grønar og gular og svartar
glampandi svartar

ongin reyður bóltur rurar seg sjálvan í blund innast í hornum
har elegantar standilampur við innbygdum teakborði
eiga valdið

## PICTURES

life has been dusted off
ten neat four by six pictures
in a smooth brown photo album
with golden silk string
a black and white life in shades of grey
frozen in film

she directs with style-conscious vitriol
he happily plays the stand-in in his own life
without feeling the invisible child
who steadies the currents in the air around them
terribly quiet breathing in the finest clothes
looking at pictures
so as not to forget anything about tidy lives

perhaps just then the child is in the basement waiting
for the cosmic photographer to leave
singing to themselves until they are carried
back up into the warmth
a derelict scent clinging to their clothes

the child is nowhere and everywhere and nowhere
there are no childish traces to be seen in the tidiness
no forgotten doll clinging to black metal legs
of severe teak tables with søholm vases

no lego bricks strewn lazily on the grey arabic pillows
which in real life are green and yellow and black
lustrous black

no red ball rocking itself to sleep in the corner
where elegant erect lamps with teak bases
hold sway

onki órógvar palisandur- og linoliums- og teak-
og bast-
og stores-
og voksdúka-
og lampettufriðin í filmkulissulívinum
ella smædnu inniskógvarnar
hjá tveimum ungum óunniliga vøkrum vaksnum

navnið á komfýrinum
kockums
var fyrsta orðið barnið dugdi at stava

smílandi sita tey bæði inni í myndunum
við hvør sínum leikluti
sum hon hevur givið teimum at spæla við
og einum barni
sum sjálvt skrivaði seg úr handlingini

vøkur brúðarmynd
trónar rodnandi og hábærsliga einsamøll
uppi á tolnum teakreolum
við kúgaðum bókaryggjum

ongin dópsmynd
við álvarsomum barni og prinsessukrúllu
í glasi og gyltari rammu
stendur við síðuna av nøkrum

kundi verið barnið fólk fáa sær og aftur gloyma
kundi verið barnið som kom og aldrin fór
aldrin fann sín egna leiklut í ruddiligum kulissum
ikki sum leikari
ikki sum statistur

nothing disturbs the rosewood—and linoleum—and teak—
and cork—
and net curtains—
and wax tablecloths—
and lampettes—peace in the movie set life
or the embarrassed slippers
of two young impeccably attractive adults

the brand of the stove
kockums
was the first word the child learned to spell

smiling the two of them sit inside the pictures
each with their separate roles
that the mother has given them to play with
and a child
who wrote themselves out

a beautiful wedding photo
sits enthroned and majestically alone
on the patient teak bookcase
with its massive bookends

no baptism photo
of a serious child with princess curls
in glass and golden frame
is next to anything

it could be the child that people get and forget again
it could be the child that came and never understood
never found their own role in the tidy scene
not as an actor
not as an extra

# RABARBUGREYTUR

Rabarburnar vóru ørar av gleði. Nú fór hann skjótt at koma eftir teimum aftur. Maðurin við mjúku hondunum, sum dugdu so væl at fara um tær. Taða tær so tær smakkaðu uppaftur betur. Deila røturnar so tær blivu enn fleiri og saftríkari. Mjúka hondin dugdi eisini at vera hørð og náðileys, tá ókrút skuldi skræðast upp ella drepast við vælmeinandi eitri, tí rabarburnar vóru hansara børn og stoltleiki, onki skuldi kunna órógva tær.

Hann var rabarbukongur í rabarburíki, og tær elskaðu hann, og um eina løtu fór hann enn einaferð at transformera tær til tann leskiligasta og mjúkasta og ljósareyðasta rabarbugreytin í allari verðini. Uttan eina einastu slintru, tí soleiðis dámdi henni best.

Lættliga skar hvassi knívurin rabarburnar í smábitar, sum allir vóru líka stórir. Angin av ráu saftini otaði seg spakuliga inn í nasagluggarnar á manninum og fylti hann við so nógvari sjálvgloymandi gleði, at hann eina løtu var púra vissur í, at hann var komin í rabarbuhimmiríki.

Gleðin vardi stutt. Álvarsom eygu eygleiddu hann og fingu hann at rakna við. Bønandi eygu sum mintu hann á, at hann aftur hevði gloymt seg burtur. Tí heldur ikki í kvøld fór hon at vilja vera rabarbudrotning saman við honum og barninum. Alt hetta stóð skrivað í eygunum á barninum, sum hugdi at honum. Ikki í kvøld. Vit orka ikki rabarbugreyt. Ikki seta útá. Hon kemur skjótt aftur, og tú veitst
hvat hendir tá.

Men hann flenti bara. Hann visti jú, hvussu væl henni dámdi hansara mjúka ljósareyða rabarbugreyt, tá hann stóð á

# RHUBARB STEW

The rhubarb stalks were overjoyed. Soon, he would come, the man with soft skilled hands. He would fertilize them so they would taste even better, separate the roots so they would become juicier. The soft hand could also be hard and ruthless when weeds had to be pulled or killed with well-meaning poison, because his rhubarb was his pride and joy, nothing should disturb it.

He was the rhubarb king in the rhubarb kingdom which loved him back and in a brief moment he could transform it once again into the most delicious and delicate and pink stewed rhubarb in the whole world. Without a single fiber because that is how she liked it.

Effortlessly, the sharp knife chopped the rhubarbs into small pieces of equal size. The smell of the raw juice worked its way into the man's nostrils and filled him with such a self-forgetting joy that he was certain, for a moment, that he was in rhubarb heaven.

The joy was short-lived. Serious eyes were watching him and shook him from his reverie. Pleading eyes reminding him that he had forgotten himself again. Because she would not be his rhubarb queen, not this evening, not here with him and the child. All this was written in the eyes of the child watching him. Not tonight. We don't want stewed rhubarb. Don't put the pot on the stove. She will return soon and you know what will happen then.

But he just laughed. He knew perfectly well how much she liked his soft pink stewed rhubarb when it was on the table without

borðinum uttan eina einastu slintru, sum kundi órógva hana.
Tí vildi hann eisini í kvøld taka øðina við, sjálvt um hann sá
óttan í eygunum á barninum og kendi tað dunkandi lítla hjartað
gjøgnum gólvið í sínum egna hjarta. Men kanska fór hon ikki
at blíva so óð í kvøld. Kanska fór alt nú at broytast. Kanska fóru
hann og barnið at klára at rudda alt upp eftir sær, so hon slettis
ikki varnaðist, at tey høvdu brúkt køkin móti hennara vilja. Tað
høvdu tey klárað onkuntíð fyrr.

Treiskliga murrandi rørdi hann í reyðu sevjuni, meðan barnið
helt ondini og fleiri ferðir helt seg hoyra hurðina ganga. Angin
av vanilju og heitari rabarbusaft nam við barnið, men angin var
ikki barnsins at njóta, heldur ikki í kvøld. Barnið kendi bara
søta sviðan í nøsini og glóðheita ekkóið av tonkunum inni í
høvdinum.

Men hurðin mátti ganga. Kalda lotið fór gjøgnum húsið og
órógvaði heita angan, so hann fann sær aðrar, hvassari leiðir.
Ein sleiv endaði á gólvinum í einum rúkandi reyðum hyli.
Endiliga steðgaði hann á og sá óruddið og osan og ákærandi
barnaeyguni. Hann hugdi tvørtur ígjøgnum barnið, svølgdi
beiska smakkin, andaði djúpt inn og gjørdi seg til reiðar. Óróliga
smílandi fór hann móti henni, beint sum hon steig inn í køkin.
Hey góða elskaða …, tey vildu jú bara gera hana glaða við
greytinum. Men smílið rein ikki við. Gjørdi bara ilt verri.

Kaldliga hugdi hon at teimum. Hon var skuffað og særd. Hann
hevði aftur víst henni, at hann ikki elskaði hana. At hann bara
vildi niðurgera hana. Vísa henni at hon ikki var líka røsk sum
hann, tí hon ikki orkaði líka væl sum hann at vera húsmóðir.
Sum hon vildi ynskt, at barnið var eitt annað barn, sum kundi
vart hana, elskað hana, og sum hon kundi elskað treytaleyst
afturímóti.

Hurðar smekkaðu. Lyklar snaraðust. Rópini og gráturin hersettu
aftur húsið og vunnu skjótt á heita anganum av vanilju og

a single fiber to annoy her. That is why he would risk her fury again tonight, even though he could see the fear in the child's eyes and felt his own small heart beating through the floor of his chest. But maybe she wouldn't be so angry tonight. Perhaps everything would change. Maybe he and the child would succeed in washing everything up, so she wouldn't notice that they had used the kitchen against her will. They had managed a few times in the past.

Stubbornly humming he stirred the red goo while the child held their breath thinking they'd heard the door several times. The smell of vanilla and warm rhubarb reached the child but didn't give them joy, not tonight. The child felt the sweet itch in their nose and the red-hot echo of the thoughts in their head.

But the door was bound to open. A cold breeze went through the house disturbing the warm scent, turning it in other sharper directions. A spoon fell to the floor in a steaming red puddle. Finally he stopped and saw the mess and smoking burner and the accusing child eyes. He looked straight past the child, swallowed the bitter taste, breathed deeply and prepared himself. He went towards her smiling uneasily, just as she stepped into the kitchen. Hello darling… we only wanted to surprise you with the rhubarb. But smiles had no effect. Only made bad worse.

She looked at them coldly. She was disappointed and hurt. Yet again, he'd showed her that he didn't love her. That he only wanted to demean her. Show her that she was not as good as he was, because she didn't have the same proclivity to be a housewife as he had. She wished the child was a different child that could protect her, love her, and that she could love back unconditionally.

Doors slammed. Keys turned. Shouting and crying once again ran through the house and overpowered the warm smell of

rabarbusaft. Og so misti hann endiliga pippið. Nú var tað aftur hann, sum hugdi bønandi at barninum. Og barnið orkaði tað ikki, slettis ikki, men fór tungliga gangandi tey somu søkkandi fetini yvir til stongdu hurðina. Enn kendi barnið ongar aðrar leiðir at fara.

Gráturin hinumegin fór beint í harða klumpin í búkinum og spenti hann uppaftur harðari. Barnið mannaði seg upp sum so ofta fyrr, svølgdi og svølgdi treiska klíggið og spurdi við mjúkari rødd, um tað kundi sleppa inn at hjálpa henni. Tey elskaðu hana bæði so høgt.

Barnið visti at bar tað til at sleppa inn í andaleysa myrkrið hinumegin hurðina, so fór alt tað ringa, sum hann hevði gjørt henni, at verða borað inn í høvdið á barninum. Hon fór eisini at krevja, at barnið ikki blundaði, men hugdi og hugdi at bláu merkjunum á kroppinum, sum hann hevði givið henni, tí hann var Dr. Jekyll og Mr. Hyde. Teir kendi barnið ikki, men barnið visti væl, at bláu merkini ikki vóru av hansara ávum, tey komu altíð, tá hann royndi at halda henni út frá sær, tá hon leyp á hann við knívi.

Og aftan á eina alt ov langa løtu fór hon knappliga at renna barnið úr aftur kamarinum, og hurðin fór aftur at blíva stongd væl og virðiliga.

Barnið ynskti og bønaði til, at tað enn einaferð bara fóru at vera teir somu eiðirnir og tey somu forbannilsini hinumegin stongdu hurðina, sum sendu tað út aftur í køkin, har hann nú sat og vaggaði aftur og fram við sleivini í munninum og royndi at fáa søta og góða smakkin at taka broddin av villareiðini. Barnið hugsaði hvør hann beint tá mundi vera, Dr. Jekyll ella hin, Mr. Hyde, og bleiv standandi hjá honum uttan at siga nakað, uttan at førka seg. Heilt ósjónligt.

vanilla and rhubarb juice. And then he finally lost it. Now he was the one to look pleadingly at the child. And the child could not stand it, not at all, but walked the heavy rickety steps to the locked door. The child didn't yet know any other place to go.

The crying on the other side of the door went directly into the hard knot in their stomach and tightened it even more. The child steeled themselves as they'd so often had to do in the past, swallowed and swallowed the stubborn sense of nausea and asked with a soft voice if they could come inside and help her. They both loved her so much.

The child knew that if they succeeded in gaining entry into the spiritless dark beyond the door, then all the wrong that he had done to her would be drilled into the child's head. She would also demand that the child never close its eyes, but look and look at the bruises on her body that he had given her, because he was both Dr. Jekyll and Mr. Hyde. The child didn't know which he was but knew the bruises weren't from him; they always happened when he tried to keep her at bay when she came at him with a knife.

And after a too long moment she would suddenly throw the child out of the room again and the door would be double latched again.

The child wished and prayed that once again there would only be the same curses and blinding beyond the locked door, that sent them back into the kitchen where he now sat rocking back and forth with the spoon in his mouth trying to get the sweet and lovely taste to take the edge of his desperation. The child wondered who he might be right then, Dr. Jekyll or the other one, Mr. Hyde, and stood standing with him without saying anything, without moving. Completely invisible.

Rópini um at hann krógvaði seg aftan fyri eitt lítið barn sum ein feikur fani og var betri við barnið enn við hana, vildu ikki fara úr aftur køkinum. Hann hugdi skuffaður og ráðaleysur upp á barnið, sum visti, at heldur ikki hesa ferð hevði tað klárað uppgávuna at blíðka hana aftur. Sum visti, at tað aftur hesa ferð hevði svikið. Og kanska fór hann ikki at orka enn eina vøkunátt í kjallaranum undir køkinum. Hvussu nógvar fór hann at orka aftrat? Áðrenn ...! Áðrenn hvat? Barnið tordi ikki at hugsa tankan lidnan.

Rabarburnar niðri í grýtuni hildu ondini, og tær hildu allar, at tað var so synd í honum. Fyri at hjálpa honum avgjørdu tær, at tær aftur hesa ferð skuldu smakka betur enn nakrantíð áður. Rabarburnar úti í havanum høvdu longu kent søta heita angan, sum knappliga bleiv hvassur, og høvdu hugsað sítt.

Tríggjar dagar seinni ótu tey øll trý tann deiliga ljósareyðasta rabarbugreytin. Hann, hon og barnið. Og láturin fór varisliga millum tey, og greyturin kitlaði vælindið so eydnuríkt vælsignað. Hon kundi ikki fáa nokk av tí himmalska smakkinum og anganum og litinum og elskaði hann fyri at duga so væl at kóka rabarbugreytin akkurát sum hon vildi hava hann.

Úti í havanum suffaðu rabarburnar av lætta og hugsaðu enn einaferð sítt.

The shouts that he hid behind a small child like a fucking coward and loved the child more than her would not leave the kitchen. He looked at the child disappointed and perplexed, who knew that they'd been unsuccessful in pacifying her yet again. That knew that they had failed again. And maybe he would not be able to stand another sleepless night in the basement under the kitchen. How many more could he stand? Before …! Before what? The child didn't dare finish the thought.

The rhubarb in the pot waited, anxious. It felt for him. To help him, it decided that it would taste better than ever. The rhubarb in the garden had already smelled the sweet warm smell turned sharp and shared the secret between them.

Three days later, the three of them ate the pinkest most delicious stewed rhubarb. He, she, and the child. And laughter moved cautiously between them and the rhubarb tickled their palates, now so fortunately blessed. She could not get enough of the heavenly taste and the smell and color and loved him for being so good at making stewed rhubarb just the way she liked it.

In the garden, the rhubarb sighed a sigh of relief and once again shared their secret.

# MÁNI

tá amerikanarar settu neil armstrong á mánan
vístu sín einaveldisrætt á jørðini
setti ein flytibilur í eysturbýnum í fyrsta gir
og koyrdi vestur um býin

í stýrhúsinum
hann og
barnið
flytimaðurin og útvarpið

sigurstolta amerikanska røddin bar boðini
beint tá vóru tey partur av eini heimsumfatandi fylking
sum var saman um løgnu hendingina
meðan hon hendi
beint tá hon hendi

smílini hitaðu andlitini
tey loyvdu sær eina kenslu av framtíðaráræði og
fanansaktigheit
beint tá
beint har
á forsetrinum í bensinstinkandi flytibilinum
teirra heilt egna rúmdarfar

kanska fór alt at laga seg álíkavæl
kanska
kanska fór alt at bera til
ein nýggj byrjan
og amerikanarar vístu vegin

ein fysiskur ómøguleiki var blivin veruleiki
nú

## MOON

when the americans put neil armstrong on the moon
and showed their supremacy over the earth
a moving van in the east of the city was dropped in gear
and driven west across town

in the front seat
he and
the child
the mover and the radio

the proud american voice delivered the message
just then they were part of a united world
that just participated in this strange event together
as it happened
the exact moment it happened

smiles heated their faces
they enjoyed a devil-may-care feeling of future courage
just then
just there
in the front seat of a van that reeked of gasoline
their very own spacecraft

perhaps everything would be all right anyway
perhaps
perhaps everything would be possible
a new beginning
and the americans would lead the way

a physical impossibility had become reality
now

nú fór eisini at bera til hjá teimum
hann kendi tað á sær
nú
nú fóru tey at skapa sær eina nýggja tilveru
rætta tilveru

tey trý
hann og hon
og
barnið

hann mátti hugsa so

barnið visti betur
ein vitan ið var
sum svongd
sum tosti
sum angist
sum
sum var ein partur av at vera ein partur av somu nervaskipan
í níggju mánaðir

ein vitan ið var ment og fínpussað alt tað stutta lívið
sum barnið kendi
barnið flenti bara við honum
í honum
móti honum
unti honum hesa løtuna í berari býttari eydnu

stásiligu húsini vestan fyri øll mørk bíðaðu bara eftir teimum
honum og henni
og barninum

náttin bar sjúkurnar í sær
fossandi blóð og pína vístu honum og barninum
at í teirra lítlu verð hevði hon einaveldisrættin

now things would also be possible for them
he could feel it
now
now they would also create a new life for themselves
a right life

the three of them
he and she
and
the child

he had to think like that

the child knew better
a knowledge that was
like hunger
like thirst
like fear
like
like a part of being a part of the same nervous system
for nine months

a knowledge developed and tuned over the whole
of the child's brief lifetime

the child just laughed with him
into him
against him
allowed him this moment of sheer foolish bliss

west of all borders the grand house waited for them
him and her
and the child

the nights brought sickness
gushing blood and pain showed him and the child

at brúka út um øll mørk fyri at halda demonunum burturi
sum búðu í verðini rundan um tey
í honum
í barninum

aldrin
í henni

av og á krøkti verðin seg upp í tey
fylgdi býtt flennandi við honum og barninum
heim til stongdu hurðarnar

verðin var ikki nóg treisk
bleiv turkað so dyggiliga av teimum
undan teimum
á mottunum
áðrenn tey sluppu inn um gáttirnar
bara tey
hann
og barnið

altumfevnandi mottur við hvørja gátt
allastaðni
bara eftirburður av teirra lofnaða sambandi við verðina
uttanfyri
sást nakrantíð á teimum
tey sporini kámaðust so við og við burtur
heilt burtur

tá amerikanarar settu seg á mánan aðru ferð
var hennara einaveldisrættur vorðin fullkomin
í stóru húsunum sum vórðu verandi nýggj í allar ævir

tíðindini um enn eina amerikanska stórhending
fóru framvið honum
og barninum

that in their little world she wielded power
beyond all reasonable limits to keep away the demons
that lived in the world around them
in him
in the child

never
in her

sometimes the world hooked itself onto them
followed the child and him idiotically laughing
home to the locked doors

the outside world didn't stick
and wiped off
on the mats
before they were allowed to cross threshold
just them
he
and the child
all-encompassing floormats at every threshold
everywhere

only the afterbirth of their numb connection to the outside world
was ever visible on them
and those traces faded gradually
then completely

when the americans landed on the moon the second time
her supremacy was complete
in the grand house that remained new for all eternity

the news of a second american triumph
escaped him
and the child

óviðkomandi tutl frá eini verð
ið aldrin rættiliga hevði verið teirra
at eiga og elska

mánin var aftur bara máni
har í húsunum

insignificant whispering of a world
that was never truly theirs
to own and love

there in the house
the moon was just the moon again

# SÓL

sólin er bannað í summum húsum
svartar rullugardinur og persiennur gera sína skyldu
sum smáir illsintir tænastumenn fyri várharra
myrkaleggja alt og øll sum látast at liva eitt vanligt lív
í húsum við ongum sólargeislum
NASA kundi ikki gjørt tað betur í sínum royndum
at halda skaðiligar geislar burturi úr himmalhválvinum

í summum húsum fylla tey seg við vitaminum í staðin
lurta eftir pressuni frá morgni til myrkurs
allan sólarringin á tamb tá andin er yvir teimum
hoyra um hungursneyð
turk
bumbumenn
bardagar
allar hugsandi vanlukkur
prísa seg lukkulig yvir at liva í einum landi
ið ikki hevur uppiborið slíkar vanlagnur
tá er tað so nógv lættari
at finna seg í síni heilt egnu lítlu vanlagnu

í myrkaløgdum húsum
sjálvt um barnið ræðist myrkrið
og ikki skilur at tað er verðin
sum hevur alla skyldina

## SUN

the sun is banned from some houses
blackout curtains and blinds do their duty
like small angry servants of our lord
who darken each and everyone pretending to live a normal life
in houses without sunbeams
NASA could not do better in its attempts
to keep away damaging rays from the heavens

in some houses they stuff themselves with vitamins instead
listening to the news from dawn to dusk
from sunrise to sunset when the spirit is upon them
hearing about famine
drought
bombs
war
every imaginable catastrophe
and count their blessings to live in a country
too innocent to deserve such misfortunes

it's so much easier
to bear one's own little misfortune
in a darkened house
even though the child is afraid of the dark
and doesn't understand it's the world
that's to blame

# SJÁLVMORÐIÐ

sjálvmorðið lakkar paradís við barninum
spælir krógva og blunda
melda kríggj
gevið ljóð
henniover ...

tað er tí tað er so lúnskt at spæla við
sjálvmorðið
barnið veit aldrin um mann kann rokna við tí
um hetta fer at verða dagurin
náttin
har orðið verður ført út í orð
tað veit bara hon sum eigur orðið
hon sum eisini er ein mamma

heldur ikki hann sum eisini er ein pápi
veit
men hann dugir av og á at reka sjálvmorðið
inn í myrkar krókar har ongin sær tað
so friður er eina løtu

ljóðini koma álíkavæl krúpandi eftir gólvunum
vilja ikki lata seg køva
vilja nema barnið
bara nema so varliga
so barnið ikki skal ræðast

tí tá verður alt verri
nógv verri
so ringt
at vandi er fyri at hon kann finna uppá

## THE SUICIDE

the suicide plays hopscotch with the child
plays hide and seek
plays war
calls out
red rover red rover

that's why it is so sneaky to play with
the suicide
the child never knows if you can count on it
if this will be the day
the night
where the word will be true to its word
only she who owns the word knows
she who also is a mother

nor does he who also is a father
know
but sometimes he knows how to drive the suicide
into dark corners where no one can see it
so that there's peace for a while

sounds still come creeping along the floor
will not be put off
want to touch the child
with a cautious touch
so the child won't be frightened

because then everything would be worse
much worse
so much worse
there is a danger that she might try

at seta seg til dómara yvir lívi og deyða
alt hetta veit barnið
alt ov nógv veit barnið

altíð
alla tíðina

hann veit ikki líka nógv
vil gjarna
roynir
men ræðist barnið

sjálvmorðið spælir sær enn einaferð veg úr trongu krókunum
fer ýlandi gjøgnum húsini
fult av gleði
bjóðar upp til dans
villan dans í náttini sum brennir allar brýr

tað veit barnið onki um
letur seg syfta við g-ferð millum hann
og hana

í nátt dansa øll aftur við tí helvitis ferð
í morgin skal sjálvmorðið sita barnagenta
heima hjá barninum
tí hann og hon
hava brúk fyri frískari luft

sjálvmorðið tekur kvørkratak um barnið
biður lova sær at sleppa at vera við
í øllum sum barnið skal uppliva
frameftir
aftureftir

í allar ævir

to become the judge over life and death
all this the child knows
the child knows too much

always
all the time

he does not know as much
wants to
tries to
but fears the child

the suicide once again sneaks out of its narrow corners
goes howling through the house
full of joy
invites everyone to dance
a mad dance in nights of burning bridges

the child knows nothing about this
accepts being swung in the g-force between him
and her

tonight once again everyone will dance as fast as fuck
tomorrow the suicide will play babysitter
home with the child
because he and she
need the fresh air

the suicide takes a stranglehold on the child
asks to join in
on all of their experiences
forward
backward

forever

# ERU KOPARRØR Í HIMMIRÍKI

brúka tey koparrør longur
ella blivu tey bannað tí hon brúkti tey
at terrorisera hann við

øll kunnu læra at terrorisera við koparrørum

bið guð um eini hús í tveimum hæddum
ein mann sum læsir seg inni í kjallaranum
leitandi eftir friðleysari hvíld í einum trongum kamari
sum altíð má liggja beint undir køkinum

gloym ikki koparrørini

maðurin torir ikki at telja myrkaløgdu tímarnar
tí bannsetta sólin fer enn einaferð at taka hann á bóli
og ringa lagið má vera á tær sum aldrin fer í song

tá bardagin er av og tú enn einaferð
hevur sparkað hann inn í seg sjálvan
ella hevur lagt á hann við knívi
og hann særdur uppá likam og sál er tørnaður inn í kjallaranum
koyr so allar kranar frá
lat vatnið gnísta sín ørandi einglasang í gyltu koparrørunum

gloym heldur ikki at skola øll vesini niður í senn
so himmalski demonurin kann surkla í sisternum
uttan íhald

køkurin er hæddarpunktið
lat kranan hvessa sítt spíska glarspjót móti stálvaskinum
koyr endiliga ikki ov hart
frá lat vatnstráluna vera akkurát so mønustingandi hvassa
at hon verður mest óúthaldilig

## ARE THERE COPPER PIPES IN HEAVEN

do they use copper pipes anymore
or are they banned because she used them
to terrorize him

anyone can learn to use copper pipes to terrorize someone

beg god for a two-story house
a man who locks himself in the basement
looking for fugitive rest in a narrow room
right beneath the kitchen

don't forget the copper pipes

the man doesn't dare count the darkened hours
because the banished sun will surprise him again
and you must always be ill-tempered and insomniac

when the fight is finished and you've once again
beat him back into himself
or have attacked him with a knife
and he wounded in body and soul has gone to sleep in the basement
turn on all the faucets
let the water creak its dizzying angel song through golden copper pipes
and don't forget to flush all the toilets at the same time
so that the heavenly demon will gurgle in the cisterns
unceasingly

the kitchen is the grand finale
let the faucet sharpen its glass-shard spear on the steel sink
please don't turn it up too much
let the water stream spine-snappingly sharp
so it becomes unbearable

óundansleppilig
beint yvir høvdinum á honum
sum enn trilvar eftir náðileysu hvíldini

metalbeinini á stólunum bíða ótolin
drag tey aftur og fram eftir gólvinum
tannapínugríslandi móti linoliinum
umaftur og umaftur
og umaftur
alla náttina

endiliga alla hesa friðsælu nátt
sum tú orkar so væl

pallmyndin er sett
tín himmalska pallmynd
nú stendur til tín
og endaleysu metrarnar av trongu koparrørunum
millum skins og hold
og niðri í gólvinum um alt húsið
at gera munin
fáa vatnið at syngja tað heilt rætta
ófrættakenda lagið
so deiliga
so óendaliga syrgið fyri oyrunum
á honum
sum liggur og starir upp undir loftið í kamarinum
beint undir tær og køkinum
við stórum turrum eygum
og ikki dugir at spyrja
hví
í tí eyguni søkka upp í ein stadnaðan harpiksblett
og gloyma tankarnar um barnið
sum liggur einsamalt uppi millum koparrørini og syngur fyri at minnast

alt

unavoidable
just over the head of the man
who is still fumbling for a pitiless sleep

the chair's restless metal feet are waiting too
drag them across the floor
teeth-grindingly against the linoleum
again and again
and again
all night

do it all night long
you're up to the task

the stage is set
your heavenly stage
it's all down to you now
you and the countless yards of thin copper pipe
inside the walls
and beneath the floorboards of the house
to set the balance
make the water sing just the right
ominous tune
so lovely
so endlessly sad to the ears
his ears
as he lies awake staring at the ceiling
just below you and the kitchen
his big dry eyes
unable to ask
why
as they sink into a stiffened resin flux on the wooden ceiling
and he forgets any thought of the child
who is lying alone in between the copper pipes
singing to themselves so they will remember

everything

## OSTASKORPUR

onkur blakar ostaskorpur út til hundin undir køksvindeyganum
reytt voks við gulum ostaleivdum
í grønum grasi
eitt glansbílæt í skeivum litum

men barnið kom fyrst
stillføra barnið
sum ongin dugir ordiliga við
heldur ikki hundurin
sum ikki fekk ostaskorpu tann dagin

tí barnið er sum ongin
og ongin ger vaksin og hundar ótrygg
fær tey at gloyma
at einsamøll børn kanska eisini
eru eydnurík børn
eina evarska lítla løtu

meðan barnið í grønum saftríkum grasi
pilkar gular ostaleivdir av reyðum voksskorpum
og njótilsið nertir allar streingir í lítla kroppinum
síggja tey vaksnu bara hundin sum onki fær

## CHEESE RINDS

someone is throwing cheese rinds to the dog beneath the
kitchen window
red wax with yellow cheese residue
in green grass
a glossy picture with all the wrong colors

but the child gets there first
the quiet child
the one nobody knows how to handle
not even the dog
who didn't get any cheese rinds that day

because the child is like a no-one
and no-ones make adults and dogs uneasy
makes them forget
that solitary children
may also be happy children
for a very short while

while the child in the lush green grass
picks bits of yellow cheese off red wax rinds
feeling pleasure thrum through their small body
the adults only see the dog who gets nothing

## 13 ÁR

ongin at tosa við um alt sum ikki ber til at siga
um onki sum aldrin vil sigast
bara leonard cohen

svart vinyl
malandi runt og runt fyri eygunum
sum ikki vilja skilja alt
sum ikki skal skiljast

reyður plátuspælari úr plastik
orðini hjá leonard raka teg beint har
sum orð skulu raka

tú ert hansara
í myrkrinum á skúmgummimadrassuni
sum spakuliga venar seg
undir hansara rødd

leonard ansar eftir tær
sendir tær hulin orð
tú bara skilur við ráa instinktinum

hann er tín meðan tú bløðir angist tí tey vaksnu hinumegin
veggin
aftur hava gloymt at vera vaksin

*and my father's hand was trembling*
*with the beauty of the world*

røddin ber teg inn í náttina
vinnur næstan á vaksna grátinum
sum hersetur tóm rúm í óendaligum húsum

## 13 YEARS

there's no one to talk with about everything that can't be said
everything that doesn't want to be said
only leonard cohen

black vinyl
spinning round and round before your eyes
that don't want to understand everything
that's not meant to be understood

the red plastic turntable
leonard's words hit you right
where words are supposed to hit

you are his
in the foam mattress dark
slowly moaning
beneath his voice

leonard watches over you
sends you coded words
that you only understand through raw instinct

he's yours while you're bleeding fear because the adults on
the other side of the wall
have forgotten to be adult again

*and my father's hand was trembling*
*with the beauty of the word*

his voice carries you into the night
almost drowning out the adult crying
that occupies empty rooms in endless houses

tú ert hansara alla náttina
meðan tú lurtar eftir fetum ið ongantíð koma
á trappum sum ongan veg føra

fremmandu orðini avdúka aldrin alt
trilvandi eftir meiningini í ómøguligum myrkri
hómandi leiklutin í leikinum
sum tú veitst tú aldrin fert at duga so væl
at spæla við í

nakrantíð

*I will help you if I must*
*I will kill you if I can*

you are his all night
as you listen for footsteps that never come
on stairs that lead to nowhere

the unfamiliar words can never show you everything
as you fumble for meaning in the impossible dark
sensing your role in the drama
and knowing you'll never be good enough
at playing it

ever

*I will help you if I must*
*I will kill you if I can*

## ISTEDGADE

horurnar og hann og hon
og barnið
peepshow á istedgade

fjákut flennandi vaksin
fornermað barn
flóvisligt at vera til

horurnar hála í hann
lokkandi varrar teska ónærisliga í oyrað á honum
sum bara dugir at flenna býtt

hon válkar sær í tí
sendir eygu full av náðileysari vanvirðing
heilt inn í tómu smurdu eyguni
sum heldur ikki síggja barnið
sum telur flisarnar beint har
á gongubreytini á istedgade

spælið er gamalt
avtalað spæl
hann vísir sær sjálvum og henni
at hann enn kann brúkast
hon fær víst hasum babylonsku skøkjunum
at hann er hennara
bara hennara

hann skal ganga fremst
hon eitt sindur aftanfyri
barnið veit
at best er at ganga allaraftast fyri ikki at gloyma
og ikki gera vart við seg

# ISTEDGADE

the whores him her
and the child
a peepshow on istedgade

silly laughing adults
a mortified child
embarrassed to be alive

the whores are pulling him
luring lips whisper luridly in his ear
and he can only laugh awkwardly

she revels in it
flashes glances of merciless contempt
boring into the painted eyes
that don't see the child either
who is counting the tiles right there
on the sidewalk of istedgade

the game is old
fixed
he shows himself and her
that he is still virile
she shows those babylonian whores
that he is hers
only hers

he must walk up front
she a little behind
the child knows
that it's best to trail behind so as not to forget
and not call attention

ikki hoyrast
ikki síggjast
ikki merkjast
bara vera

hann sigur
vit búnast seint í okkara familju
men øll eiga rættin einaferð at sleppa framat svarinum

eina løtu spæla øll spælið
einsamallur maður trolar eftir horum
hann sleppur eina løtu at spæla
at hann er frælsari enn frelsarin
til reiðar at lata girndina ráða fult og heilt í sær
vísa horunum sína megi sum mann

tær halda hann vera vakran og hábærsligan
tað veit hon at tær halda at hann er

istedgade er teirra nú
og hon er harðrendi djóratemjarin
bara hon veit nær spælið ikki er stuttligt longur

barnið steðgar jørðini
blundar
ræðist at drukna í eymleikanum
sum eina løtu hómast í smurdu eygunum
men har eru aldrin nóg nógvir óteljandi flisar at telja
knappliga tímir hon ikki at spæla longur
sveimar sigurstolt framvið glataðu kvinnuhjørtunum
sum beint tá bjóða seg fram til hansara sum bara er hennara

horurnar síggja heilt inn á botn
har lítli drongurin í honum býr
sjónin setur tær í samband við dýpið í teimum sjálvum
ger tær so veikar at hon fær dripið tær

not to be heard
not to be seen
not to be felt
just to be

he says
we mature late in our family
but everyone has the right to reach the answers sometime

for a moment everyone plays the game
single man runs after whores
he is allowed to play for a while
and he is freer than the saviour
ready to let the lust take charge of him
show the whores his power as a man

they think that he is handsome and dignified
she knows they think so

istedgade is theirs now
and she is the ruthless lion tamer
only she gets to decide when the game isn't fun anymore

the child stops the earth
eyes closed
afraid to drown in the pity
reflected for a moment in those painted eyes
but there are never enough uncountable tiles to count
suddenly she doesn't want him to play anymore
and swings triumphantly past the ruined women's hearts
who have just offered themselves to him who is only hers

the whores see all the way to the bottom
to the little boy inside him
and the vision puts them in touch with the abyss in
themselves

við dreparaeygunum
tað dugir hon so væl
ein fyri og onnur eftir liggja tær eftirá

á istedgade
avtaglað við deyðum horum
blóðið rennur í heimligum tutlandi áarløkum
dryppar niður gjøgnum rustaðu jarnristirnar
heilt niður í undirvitið á stórbýnum

hon slettir blóðið úr eygunum
barnið vassar seigliga gjøgnum blóðhyljarnar
heldur onki vera stuttligt longur
barnið visti tað altíð
onki vaksið er nakrantíð ordiliga stuttligt

longri frammi hvørva hann og hon harðliga flennandi
um hornið við vøkru tokstøðina
barnið blundar
druknar glaðiliga í øllum blóðinum
og smílist innantanna

renders them so weak she can kill them
with those killer eyes
she's so good at
one by one they fall

on istedgade
covered in dead whores
blood runs in cheery babbling brooks
dripping through rusted iron grates
all the way down into the subconscious of the metropolis

she wipes the blood from her eyes
the child trudges through the bloody pools
nothing is fun anymore
the child knew it all along
nothing grown up is ever really fun

up ahead he and she disappear laughing violently
around the corner by the beautiful train station
the child stands still with their eyes shut fast
drowning happily in all the blood
and smiling on the inside

## SKÁK OG MÁT

ímillum ár og dag lá lívið
sum ikki vildi livast
fult av sárum
sum tíðin ikki dugdi at lekja

álíkavæl gekk hjartað so trúliga
sína treisku gongd
negl og hár vuksu sínar millimetrar
sveittin lak undir ørmum
og millum bein
har eisini blóðið fann sína kós
meðan forbannilsini blómaðu
og jesus og devulin sótu undir hvørjum orði

tann kvinnan hon sá í speglinum
og í eygunum á hinum
var aldrin tann sama
sum hini sóu tá tey hugdu at henni

tað visti hon

nær kemur gleðin til mín
spurdi hon barnið
sum ikki dugdi at svara
beint tá

lívið vildi ikki taka hana
fyri fult
tímdi hon at taka lívið
fyri fult

hon visti bara
at tilveran mátti setast
skák og mát

## CHECK MATE

between a year and a day was a life
that did not want to be lived
full of wounds
that time could not heal

but the heart faithfully beat
its stubborn rhythm
nails and hair grew by millimetres
sweat perspired under arms
and between legs
where blood also found its way
while curses blossomed
and jesus and the devil listened to every word

the woman she saw reflected in the mirror
and in the eyes of other people
was never the same
as what other people saw when they looked at her

she knew that

when will joy come to me
she asked the child
who could not find an answer
just then

life would not take her
seriously
she would not take her life
seriously

she only knew
that existence must be put in
check mate

# SJÁLVMORÐIÐ

sjálvmorðið ið aldrin er
men allatíðina er har álíkavæl
sum eitt alt ov veruligt bræv
á hvøssum teppi uttan fyri eina hurð

sum ein kropslig hóttan
ovast á eini trappu við 13 trinum
sum eitt geyl út gjøgnum eitt vindeyga
ið ikki vil latast upp

sum nakin ræðsla
ið fyllir tómrúmið í einum húsum
sum andaleys gleði
ið bara kann bløða inneftir
líka til hjartað brestur
av eydnuríkari møði

## THE SUICIDE

the suicide that never is
but is nevertheless ever present
like a too-real letter
on the bristly mat outside a door

like a bodily threat
on the top of a thirteen-step staircase
like a howl out a window
that won't open

like naked horror
that fills the emptiness of a house
like breathless joy
that can only bleed internally
until the heart bursts with happy fatigue

# SMÍL

hvat krógvar seg aftan fyri smílið
spyr býtt
tankarnir for fanin
tankatómir

ikki lata teir uppdaga teg

penir tankar
harðir tankar
kaldir tankar
tankar
tankar larma so illa
tá tøgnin spælir býtt

halt kjaft ikki
hvør slepti teimum út
doyði tú frá teimum
hví tókst tú teir ikki bara við tær

sluppu teir út gjøgnum sprungurnar í tínum mishátta skølti
fyri at plága øll rundan um teg
so tú í friði og náðum kundi byrja tína óendaliga tankatómu ferð
heilt út hagar sum alt byrjar
og billa tær sjálvum inn
at tú ert ein av teimum endurføddu

gott fornøyilsi tú

á lat bara vera

## SMILE

what hides behind that smile
a stupid question
the fucking thoughts
thoughtless

don't let them find you out

pretty thoughts
hard thoughts
cold thoughts
thoughts
thoughts that are so noisy
when silence is playing dumb

god dammit
who let them out
did you die from them
why didn't you just bring them with you

did they escape through the cracks in your ugly skull
in order to torment everyone around you
allowing you to start your endless empty-headed voyage
all the way out to where everything begins
and you tell yourself
that you are one of the born-again

have a great time, man

oh just stop

## TEY DEYÐU

ikki ræðast tey deyðu áðrenn tú doyrt
tey eru bara deyð
tú ert bara á lívi

kanska stendur skrivað í loyniligum bókum
um øll hesi deyðu sum gleða seg til tú kemur
tú
bara tú
øll hesi tú nam á vegnum gjøgnum ógloymandi leikin
ið gjørdist tín

ja so er skrivað
øll hesi sum bera agg til tín
tey sum tú ikki tímdi at dansa við
tey tú onkursvegna traðkaði á tærnar við tínum balstýrigu
stálhælum
sum oftast av óvart
og við vilja

kanska bíða tey bara eftir einum kjansi at siga tær
hvussu øgiliga beistaktig tú ert
hvussu fanansliga dugnaleys tú altíð hevur verið

kanska bíða tey bara eftir at sleppa at smakka søtu hevndina
gera tær ævinleikan ótolandi
tú vart jú altíð so egin
so helvitisliga inni í tær sjálvari
afturhaldandi sum sjálv pestin
hevði ikki brúk fyri øðrum

sanniliga stendur skrivað í ósjónligum bókum
at øll tey deyðu eru har

## THE DEAD

do not fear the dead before you die
they are only dead
you are only living

maybe it is written in secret annals
the book of the dead who look forward to your arrival
you
only you
everyone that you touched along the way through the
unforgettable drama
that became your own

verily it is written
all those who carry a grudge against you
the ones you didn't want to dance with
the ones whose feet you somehow stepped on with your
truculent steel heels
mostly accidentally
sometimes on purpose

maybe they are just waiting for a chance to tell you
what a fucker you are
how fucking useless you've always been

maybe they're only waiting to taste sweet revenge
and make eternity intolerable for you
you were always so peculiar
so fucking within yourself
reserved like the plague itself
never needing anyone else

verily it is written in invisible books

kenslan av teimum er altuppetandi
tá tú traðkar um gátt gáttanna
nógv teirra eru ikki blíð
serliga mammur og pápar standa klár við ógloymdum ákærum
sum bara tú dugir innanat og uttanat

men hesaferð er ongin undanvegur
tú kanst ikki bara rýma
sleppa tær av fananum til
sum flytifuglur við einvegisbillett út í tóman heim

her bíðar ævinleikans brigsl og vreiði
og avnoktan
eftir tær
bara tær

that all the dead are there
the sense of them is all-consuming
when you step across that threshold of thresholds
many of them will not be kind
particularly mothers and fathers who stand ready with
familiar accusations
you know by heart

but this time there's no way out
you can't just run away
get the hell out of here
like a migrating bird with one-way ticket to nowhere

there await accusations and anger
eternal anger
and denial
for you
just for you

## ÚTVARP

útvarpið kringsetur heimini og heilarnar
altíð spýggjandi hart frá
allastaðni
hvønn tann einasta dag

børnini fáa matin kroystan í seg
tí børnini svølta í biafra
hjartkipt tyggja og svølgja tey seg diddarak
meðan útvarpið meylar um atombumbubrintatomvandan
og tað sum verri er

tíðindi og andlát
tónleikur uttan vit og skittfisk
doyggjandi røddir
siga frá dansi og jarðarferðum
og dunnuspæli og andláti
syftast gjøgnum vælindini saman við rotna matinum
sum aldrin verður til meiri enn eina klíggjan
hjá mammum sum ikki duga at gera mat
og pápum sum ikki orka longur
at tyggja børnini til útvarpið aftur slóknar

## RADIO

the radio besieges heart and home
always nauseatingly loud
everywhere
every single day

children have food stuffed into them
because children in Biafra are starving
terrified they chew and swallow themselves skinny as a stick
while the radio is babbling about atombomdhydrogennucleardanger
and worse

news and death reports
canned music and junk fish
dying voices
that announce dances and funerals
bingo nights and eulogies
are vomited back up the gullet with the rotten food
which never amounts to anything more than regurgitation
of mothers who don't know how to cook
and father who don't have the energy
to chew their children up before the radio fritzes out again

# LÍKAMIKIÐ

hvat er at ræðast fyri
at øll fara frá tær
at missa tíni kæru

tryggleikin
svikaligur

tankin um tankan
er hugsaður langt áðrenn hann vaknar
tí tankin svevur aldrin í tær

soleiðis var tað og er tað
í øllum teimum forpestaðu lívunum
meðan tey livast
á so fitt og elskulig
og ræðandi harðrend
og óundansleppandi deilig

líkamikið sigur tú
hvat fanin merkir tað

líkamikið
er sjálvur tankin um lívið líkamikið
hvør ert tú so
hví ert tú

## NEVERMIND

what is there to fear
that everyone will leave you
that you will lose your loved ones

never trusting
peace of mind

the thought never rests in you
the thought about the thought
that's the way it is and always was
in all the tainted lives
being lived
oh so nice and lovely
and terrifyingly violent
and inescapably wonderful

nevermind you say
what the fuck does that mean

nevermind

is there nothing else but nevermind
then who are you
why are you

# ACKNOWLEDGEMENTS

This translation was made possible by the financial support of Mentanargrunnur Landsins. I am indebted to my co-translator Sámal Soll who sat with me and hammered out a rough English version. I am also grateful for the author who worked with me via email on edits and rewrites. I am also grateful for the summer institute at Fróðskaparsetur Føroya and in particular for the kindness and support of Turið Sigurðardóttir.

These translations have appeared, in slightly different versions, in *Anomaly*, *The Arkansas International*, and *The Scores*.

# BREAKING OPEN THE LONG DARK

# A CONVERSATION WITH TRANSLATOR MATTHEW LANDRUM

*Greetings! Thank you for talking to us about your process today! Can you introduce yourself, in a way that you would choose?*

Thanks. I'm so grateful for this space. *Are there Copper Pipes in Heaven* is the second full length collection of Faroese work ever to be published in English – and am excited to share it.

*Why do you work in translation?*

I did my MFA capstone lecture on translation theory but only worked with Latin at the time – no living poets. Years later, I ended up partnering with a Faroese poet during a language study in Tórshavn. One thing led to another and I've now worked with ten different poets and writers from the islands. For a population just over 50,000, the number of great writers, visual artists, and musicians the culture produces is staggering. I translate by diving into work I admire from a culture I love and then offering it up in my own language.

*In addition or instead of "translator," what other titles or affiliations do you prefer/feel are more accurate? What other work are you doing in the world these days?*

I'm first and foremost a poet. I'm not fluent in Faroese though I have studied it. I work with a co-translator. We put our heads together on getting an English crib and then my job is to create living breathing poetry in English. This is a form of translation though it may not be the one that comes to mind for people when they hear the title translator. Coleman Barks, the great Rumi translator, doesn't speak Persian. Ted Hughes worked in a dozen language he didn't speak. So did Robert Bly. To me, the overriding question of translation is "does it recreate the poetry as poetry in the new language?" Accuracy is important but translation is an exercise in poetry not in academics.

Besides writing, I teach English and music at a high school for students with neuro-diverse learning styles (autism, ADHD, and non-verbal learning differences). I'm also a songwriter and musician. Translation dovetails with all these things nicely but the full slate means translation projects can take years. This one took three.

*Talk about the process or instinct to move this project into book form. How and why did this happen? Have you had this intention for a while? What encouraged and/or confounded this (or a book, in general) coming together?*

I do a lot of selected translating – this poem or that, often at the behest FarLit, the Faroese government literature promotion agency. This project was different. I applied for a grant to translate an entire book. And I'm glad I did. This is a book that works as a unit.

On an impossibly balmy week in August, I sat down with my co-translator, the Faroese fiction writer Sámal Soll, at his kitchen table in front of a window with a view of The Black Falls and the capital. We knocked out preliminary translations out in two afternoons. Then the book sat for a while, taking a backseat to a new school year.

In early winter, I emailed Katrin a draft and she sent back corrections and notes. I spent the next four months working to capture the vision she laid out in her emails, writing and rewriting the translations. As we went back and forth, we talked about the philosophy, trying to find a balance between music and meaning, sense and definition. This was frustrating sometimes. I rewrote the book with three sets of pronouns and tinkered and tinkered before I felt I'd matched the author's vision. This tug of war ultimately made my translations better and I'm grateful for the insights gained.

*What practices or structures (if any) do you use in the creation of your work, beyond this project? Have certain teachers or instructive environments, or readings/writings/work of other creative people informed the way you work/write?*

Writers must be readers first. I can always tell when I haven't been reading poetry because my own poetry feels stale, retracing the same rabbit trails of topic and technique. Reading deeply opens new vistas, sparks innovation, shakes us free of stuckness. Translation is the deepest form of reading I know and the practice of recreating beautiful work from Faroese in English has been a gift to my writing. Beyond this, it has helped me see life through the eyes of a different culture. Though translating doesn't make me Faroese and I can't fully grasp or inhabit that space, the process has given me so much beauty and new sight.

*What does this particular work represent to you both as indicative of your method/creative practice? as indicative of your history? as indicative of your mission/intentions/hopes/plans?*

Other translation projects have been quietly queueing behind this one. Others are queueing behind those. I don't imagine I'll ever catch up, but it's a happy problem to have. Now that this is finished, I plan to finish translating The Sun's Taste by Rannvá Holm Mortensen, a book I fell in love with while doing an excerpt for FarLit.

*What does this book DO (as much as what it says or contains)?*

This book break privacy taboos in Faroese culture. It's very controversial and many people I talked to expressed doubts about whether or not it should have been written in the first place. In English, confessional poetry is common. In Faroese, it's never been done before. In a society where people know each other or are separated by a single degree of acquaintance, privacy as at a premium and people guard theirs. Breaking open the side of a house and exposing its darkness – abuse, neglect, mental illness, drug use, suicide – goes against the grain. It's difficult subject matter and Ottarsdóttir makes it hard to miss. A consummate filmmaker, she also explored the material of this book in a feature film and an interactive art exhibit. Her work – in film, art, and poetry here – brings these issues into the public sphere in a way that hasn't been done before in Faroese culture.

*What would be the best possible outcome for this book? What might it do in the world, and how might its presence as an object facilitate your creative role in your community and beyond? What are your hopes for this book, and for your practice?*

The Faroe Islands, in the colonial shadow of The Kingdom of Denmark, is obscure to most people. When I say I translate Faroese poetry, it usually leads to a ten-minute explanation of where the islands are and how I came to them. I'd like more people to know about the Faroes and experience them through literature.

*Let's talk a little bit about the role of translation, creative practice and community in social and political activism, so present in our daily lives as we face the often sobering, sometimes dangerous realities of the Capitalocene. How does your process, practice, or work otherwise interface with these conditions?*

A few hundred years ago, the population of the islands was around 5,000. Danish was the official language of religion, commerce, and education. The elite of the capital spoke Danish. Priests were imported from Denmark. But the center of Faroese life communal dances. In the streets during mild summer evenings or in village halls or houses during the long winter dark, people would join hands in a chain and step twice to the left and once to the right. Their feet their only accompaniment, they would join in singing ancient ballads stretching back to Germanic paganism. It was the center of native culture, a chance to get a break from rural isolation, to see friends and eat good food. This interior life of Faroese culture protected and propagated the language from outside forces.

When Romanticism came to the Faroes, writing poetry and music in the vernacular became a form of resistance against Danish colonialism. Ballads were studied and recorded and their ancient roots were recognized. Faroese, long seen as a backwater dialect of Danish, was now viewed as truer to the Old Norse roots. Writing was an act of defiance.

Choosing to write in a language only 65,000 people can read continues to be a way of claiming Faroeseness against outside pressure. That pressure now comes mainly from the anglophone world where advertising, mass media, and technology reach into pockets. Young Faroese people are saying things like *vit skypast* and *eg googla*. Organizers changed Føroysku Tónlistavirðislønirnar to The Faroese Music Awards (FMAs). Capitalism asks people to be homogeneous consumer. Katrin Ottarsdóttir could write in Danish or even English. She lives in Copenhagen and is involved with its vibrant arts and film scene. Danish would open doors. But she chooses to write about her childhood in the language of her childhood. This is an vulnerability and resistance.

At its most basic level, translation is deep reading. It's intimate, something akin to love. My great joy as a translator is to share what I love. And I believe it is important for people to hear. Writing is not the only act of resistance. Reading is also taking a stand against the techno-capitalist model of distraction and homogeneity. The fringe, the minority, the repressed have important things to say to the humanity. Without them we are less.

**MATTHEW LANDRUM** is the author of *Berlin Poems* (A Midsummer Night's Press). His translations from Faroese have recently appeared in *Asymptote Journal, Michigan Quarterly Review, Image,* and *Modern Poetry in Translation.* He lives in Detroit.


**SÁMAL SOLL** is a Faroese writer and translator. His short story collection *Glasbúrið* was published in 2015. He has an MA degree in English Language and Literature from Aalborg University in Denmark and has just completed a degree in Faroese Language at the Faroese University in the Faroe Islands. He is currently working on a translation of Ernest Hemingway's *In Our Time*. You can read more about his work at www.samalsoll.wordpress.com.


**KATRIN OTTARSDÓTTIR** is a pioneer in Faroese filmmaking and has made several feature films, documentaries, shorts etc., e.g. the award winning feature films *Atlantic Rhapsody* (1989), *Bye Bye Blue Bird* (1999), and *LUDO* (2014). Born 1957 in Tórshavn, Faroe Islands, she studied film directing at the National Danish Film School. She debuted as a writer in 2012 with the poetry collection *Are Copper Pipes In Heaven* (awarded the Faroese Litterature Award 2013). In 2015 she published the poetry collection *Mass For A Film*, and in 2016 a collection of short *STORIES, AFTER BEFORE.*

## GLOSSARIUM:
### UNSILENCED TEXTS AND MODERN TRANSLATIONS

The Operating System's GLOSSARIUM: UNSILENCED TEXTS series was established in early 2016 in an effort to recover silenced voices outside and beyond the canon, seeking out and publishing both contemporary translations and little or un-known out of print texts, in particular those under siege by restrictive regimes and silencing practices in their home (or adoptive) countries. We are committed to producing dual-language versions whenever possible.

Few, even avid readers, are aware of the startling statistic reporting that less than three percent of all books published in the United States, per UNESCO, are works in translation. Less than one percent of these (closer to 0.7%) are works of poetry and fiction. You can imagine that even less of these are experiemental or radical works, in particular those from countries in conflict with the US or where funding is hard to come by.

Other countries are far, far ahead of us in reading and promoting international literature, a trend we should be both aware of and concerned about—how does it come to pass that our attentions become so myopic, and as a result, so under-informed? We see the publication of translations, especially in volume, to be a vital and necessary act for all publishers to require of themselves in the service of a more humane, globally aware, world. By publishing 7 titles in 2019, we increased the number of translated books of literature published in the US last year *by a full percent.* We plan to continue this growth as much as possible.

The dual-language titles either in active circulation or forthcoming in this series include Arabic-English, Farsi-English, Polish-English, French-English, Faroese-English, Yaqui Indigenous American translations, and Spanish-English translations from Cuba, Argentina, Mexico, Uruguay, Bolivia, and Puerto Rico.

The term 'Glossarium' derives from latin/greek and is defined as 'a collection of glosses or explanations of words, especially of words not in general use, as those of a dialect, locality or an art or science, or of particular words used by an old or a foreign author.' The series is curated by OS Founder and Managing Editor Elæ [Lynne DeSilva-Johnson,] with the help of global collaborators and friends.

## WHY PRINT / DOCUMENT?

*The Operating System uses the language "print document" to differentiate from the book-object as part of our mission to distinguish the act of documentation-in-book-FORM from the act of publishing as a backwards-facing replication of the book's agentive \*role\* as it may have appeared the last several centuries of its history. Ultimately, I approach the book as TECHNOLOGY: one of a variety of printed documents (in this case,* **bound***) that humans have invented and in turn used to archive and disseminate ideas, beliefs, stories, and other evidence of production.*

*Ownership and use of printing presses and access to (or restriction of printed materials) has long been a site of struggle, related in many ways to revolutionary activity and the fight for civil rights and free speech all over the world. While (in many countries) the contemporary quotidian landscape has indeed drastically shifted in its access to platforms for sharing information and in the widespread ability to "publish" digitally, even with extremely limited resources, the importance of publication on physical media has not diminished. In fact, this may be the most critical time in recent history for activist groups, artists, and others to insist upon learning, establishing, and encouraging personal and community documentation practices. Hear me out.*

*With The OS's print endeavors I wanted to open up a conversation about this: the ultimately radical, transgressive act of creating PRINT /DOCUMENTATION in the digital age. It's a question of the archive, and of history: who gets to tell the story, and what evidence of our life, our behaviors, our experiences are we leaving behind? We can know little to nothing about the future into which we're leaving an unprecedentedly digital document trail — but we can be assured that publications, government agencies, museums, schools, and other institutional powers that be will continue to leave BOTH a digital and print version of their production for the official record. Will we?*

*As a (rogue) anthropologist and long time academic, I can easily pull up many accounts about how lives, behaviors, experiences — how THE STORY of a time or place — was pieced together using the deep study of correspondence, notebooks, and other physical documents which are no longer the norm in many lives and practices. As we move our creative behaviors towards digital note taking, and even audio and video, what can we predict about future technology that is in any way assuring that our stories will be accurately told – or told at all? How will we leave these things for the record?*

*In these documents we say:*
*WE WERE HERE, WE EXISTED, WE HAVE A DIFFERENT STORY*

*- Elæ [Lynne DeSilva-Johnson], Founder/Creative Director*
*THE OPERATING SYSTEM, Brooklyn NY 2018*

# RECENT & FORTHCOMING
## OS PRINT::DOCUMENTS and PROJECTS, 2019-20

# 2020

Institution is a Verb: A Panoply Performance Lab Compilation
Poetry Machines: Letters for a Near Future - Margaret Rhee
My Phone Lies to me: Fake News Poetry Workshops as
Radical Digital Media Literacy - Alexandra Juhasz, Ed.
Goodbye Wolf-Nik DeDominic
Spite - Danielle Pafunda
Acid Western - Robert Balun
Bloodletting - Joseph Han

## KIN(D)* TEXTS AND PROJECTS

Hoax - Joey De Jesus
#Survivor - Joanna C. Valente
Intergalactic Travels: Poems from a Fugutive Alien - Alan Pelaez Lopez
RoseSunWater - Angel Dominguez

## GLOSSARIUM: UNSILENCED TEXTS AND TRANSLATIONS

Are There Copper Pipes in Heaven - Katrin Ottarsdóttir
(Faroe Islands, trans. Matthew Landrum)
Zugunruhe - Kelly Martinez Grandal (tr. Margaret Randall)
En el entre / In the between: Selected Antena Writings -
Antena Aire  (Jen Hofer &  John Pluecker)
Black and Blue Partition ('Mistry) - Monchoachi (tr. Patricia Hartland)
Si la musique doit mourir (If music were to die) -
Tahar Bekri (tr. Amira Rammah)
Farvernes Metafysik: Kosmisk Farvelære (The Metaphysics of Color:
A Cosmic Theory of Color) - Ole Jensen Nyrén (tr. Careen Shannon)
Híkurí (Peyote)  - José Vincente Anaya (tr. Joshua Pollock)
Unnatural Bird Migrator - Ariel Resnikoff

# 2019

Ark Hive-Marthe Reed
I Made for You a New Machine and All it Does is Hope - Richard Lucyshyn
Illusory Borders-Heidi Reszies
A Year of Misreading the Wildcats - Orchid Tierney
Of Color: Poets' Ways of Making | An Anthology of Essays on
Transformative Poetics - Amanda Galvan Huynh &
Luisa A. Igloria, Editors
Collaborative Precarity Bodyhacking Work-Book and Guide -
Lynne DeSilva-Johnson / ELÆ, Cory Tamler & Storm Budwig

## KIN(D)* TEXTS AND PROJECTS

A Bony Framework for the Tangible Universe-D. Allen
Opera on TV-James Brunton
Hall of Waters-Berry Grass
Transitional Object-Adrian Silbernagel

## GLOSSARIUM: UNSILENCED TEXTS AND TRANSLATIONS

Śnienie / Dreaming - Marta Zelwan/Krystyna Sakowicz,
(Poland, trans. Victoria Miluch)
High Tide Of The Eyes - Bijan Elahi (Farsi-English/dual-language)
trans. Rebecca Ruth Gould and Kayvan Tahmasebian
In the Drying Shed of Souls: Poetry from Cuba's Generation Zero
Katherine Hedeen and Víctor Rodríguez Núñez, translators/editors
Street Gloss - Brent Armendinger
with translations of Alejandro Méndez, Mercedes Roffé,
Fabián Casas, Diana Bellessi, and Néstor Perlongher (Argentina)
Operation on a Malignant Body - Sergio Loo
(Mexico, trans. Will Stockton)

# DOC U MENT
## /däkyəmənt/

First meant "instruction" or "evidence," whether written or not.

*noun* - a piece of written, printed, or electronic matter that provides information or evidence or that serves as an official record
*verb* - record (something) in written, photographic, or other form
*synonyms* - paper - deed - record - writing - act - instrument

[*Middle English, precept, from Old French, from Latin documentum, example, proof, from docre, to teach; see dek- in Indo-European roots.*]

### Who is responsible for the manufacture of value?

Based on what supercilious ontology have we landed in a space where we vie against other creative people in vain pursuit of the fleeting credibilities of the scarcity economy, rather than freely collaborating and sharing openly with each other in ecstatic celebration of MAKING?

While we understand and acknowledge the economic pressures and fear-mongering that threatens to dominate and crush the creative impulse, we also believe that *now more than ever we have the tools to relinquish agency via cooperative means,* fueled by the fires of the Open Source Movement.

Looking out across the invisible vistas of that rhizomatic parallel country we can begin to see our community beyond constraints, in the place where intention meets resilient, proactive, collaborative organization.

Here is a document born of that belief, sown purely of imagination and will. When we document we assert. We print to make real, to reify our being there. When we do so with mindful intention to address our process, to open our work to others, to create beauty in words in space, to respect and acknowledge the strength of the page we now hold physical, a thing in our hand, we remind ourselves that, like Dorothy: *we had the power all along, my dears.*

### THE PRINT! DOCUMENT SERIES
*is a project of*
the trouble with bartleby
*in collaboration with*
**the operating system**

www.ingramcontent.com/pod-product-compliance
Lightning Source LLC
Chambersburg PA
CBHW022010120526
44592CB00034B/769